Hooray for Hollywood *Cocktails!*

50 LEGENDARY DRINKS INSPIRED BY TINSELTOWN'S BIGGEST STARS

Katherine Bebo

with photography by Alex Luck

DOG 'N' BONE

For Lynn. Hooray for you!

Senior designer Emily Breen
Editor Kate Reeves-Brown
Writer Katherine Bebo
Head of production Patricia Harrington
Art director Sally Powell
Creative director Leslie Harrington
Editorial director Julia Charles

Published in 2024 by Dog 'n' Bone (Cico) Books
An imprint of Ryland Peters & Small
20–21 Jockey's Fields
London WC1R 4BW
and
341 E 116th St
New York, NY 10029

www.rylandpeters.com

10 9 8 7 6 5 4 3 2 1

Recipe collection compiled by Katherine Bebo.
Text copyright © Julia Charles, Jesse Estes, Ursula Ferrigno, Laura Gladwin, Ben Reed,
David T. Smith, Keli Rivers and Cico Books 2024. See page 64 for full credits.
Design and photography copyright © Cico Books 2024.
AdobeStock.com: by ONYXprj, Glay and Emas.

A CIP catalog record for this book is available from the British Library
and the US Library of Congress.

ISBN 978-1-912983-82-7

Printed in China

CONTENTS

Steal the Scene with these Star-Studded Sips

James Bond requesting his martini be shaken, not stirred. The Dude knocking back his milky White Russians in *The Big Lebowski*. Carrie Bradshaw clinking her fabulous Cosmopolitans with her best friends in *Sex and the City*. Indeed, the silver screen is abuzz with cocktails – and here we raise a glass to them all.

It's not just the obvious pairings of celebrity and cocktail that you'll find in *Hooray for Hollywood Cocktails*! There are also some more subtle connections to team each drink with its relevant Hollywood star. Enter Matt Damon with an Appletini, Marilyn Monroe with a Sweet Manhattan and Meryl Streep with an El Diablo.

Whether you're using Oscar-worthy whiskey, va-va-voom vodka, Tinseltown tequila, red-carpet rum or glitterati gin to mix up a dramatic drink, this collection of bold blockbuster beverages will receive rave reviews from you and your movie-loving amigos. Amongst the martinis, negronis, sour sips, zingy tipples, fruity numbers and dessert cocktails, you'll find more pizzazz than you would at an Oscars after-party.

Whatever you have a hankering for, you're invited to pore over the following 50 razzmatazz recipes, then pour yourself a lip-smacking libation that belongs in the limelight as much as its corresponding A-lister.

Sip, sip, hooray!

CHAPTER 1

Movie Martinis

Vesper Martini

Daniel Craig in Casino Royale

WHEN THE SUAVE BOND ORDERS A DRY
MARTINI (LATER NAMED A VESPER MARTINI
AFTER THE VIVACIOUS VESPER LYND)
DURING A TENSE POKER GAME IN *CASINO
ROYALE*, HIS OPPONENTS THINK IT
SOUNDS SO TEMPTING THAT THEY
ORDER ONE TOO.

Shake the ingredients vigorously with ice. Serve
in a pre-chilled cocktail glass garnished with
a delicate twist of lemon peel.

60 ml/2 oz. Gordon's
Gin Travellers' Edition
(47.3% ABV)

20 ml/⅔ oz.
grain-based vodka

10 ml/⅓ oz. Kina Lillet
(a 50:50 mix of Lillet
Blanc and China Martini
is a great substitute)

twist of lemon peel,
to garnish

Serves 1

Dirty Martini

Clint Eastwood in Dirty Harry

50 ml/1¾ oz. potato vodka (such as Royal Mash) or Gin Eva olive gin

5 ml/¼ oz. dry vermouth (Vault Coastal is particularly good)

5–15 ml/¼–½ oz. green olive brine

3 green olives, to garnish

Serves 1

"THERE WERE A LOT OF REASONS THEY CALLED HIM DIRTY HARRY, AND HE KEPT INVENTING NEW ONES." JOIN LOOSE CANNON DETECTIVE HARRY CALLAHAN IN HIS RECKLESS WAYS AS YOU GET STUCK INTO THIS DOWN-AND-DIRTY MARTINI.

Combine all the ingredients in a cocktail shaker with ice and shake vigorously. Strain into a cocktail glass and garnish with 3 olives.

GIBSON MARTINI

For an equally (un)savoury alternative, omit the olive brine and olive garnish and add a toothpick threaded with a small pearl onion to create another classic.

Pornstar Martini

Amanda Seyfried in Lovelace

DUBBED 'THE POSTER GIRL FOR THE SEXUAL REVOLUTION', LINDA LOVELACE STARRED IN THE 1972 MOVIE *DEEP THROAT*, WHICH BECAME A WORLDWIDE PHENOMENON. SWALLOW THIS SWEET, CULT COCKTAIL DOWN AS YOU FOLLOW AMANDA SEYFRIED DEPICTING THE PORNSTAR'S THRILLING JOURNEY.

Add the ingredients (except the Champagne) to a cocktail shaker with ice and shake vigorously. Strain into a coupe glass. Garnish with the passion fruit and serve at once with a shot glass of Champagne on the side.

60 ml/2 oz. vodka

15 ml/½ oz. passion fruit purée or Passoa liqueur

15 ml/½ oz. vanilla syrup

15 ml/½ oz. fresh lime juice

½ passion fruit, to garnish

a shot glass of Champagne or other sparkling wine, chilled, to serve

Serves 1

Millionaire's Martini

Leonardo DiCaprio in The Great Gatsby

50 ml/1¾ oz. Beefeater Crown Jewel Dry Gin or grain-based vodka

10 ml/⅓ oz. dry vermouth (such as Dolin)

5–10 ml/¼–⅓ oz. dry sparkling wine (such as Champagne or Crémant)

cocktail sparkler anchored by a roll of grapefruit peel, to garnish

Serves 1

DON A BLACK-TIE TUXEDO OR FLAPPER DRESS AS YOU PARTY LIKE IT'S 1922, *GREAT GATSBY*-STYLE. WITH THIS LUXE LIBATION, EXPECT POOLSIDE DANCING, FIREWORKS AND RIP-ROARING FUN. CHEERS, OLD SPORT.

Shake or stir the spirit and vermouth with ice, then fine-strain into a Champagne coupe and top up with the chilled sparkling wine.

Garnish with a small cocktail sparkler anchored by a roll of grapefruit peel.

Caution: Make sure to remove the sparkler before drinking!

NOTE: The grapefruit flavours from the Beefeater Crown Jewel provide a lively zestiness that pairs well with the dry flavours of the wines, while the slightly higher ABV gives the drink a botanical power.

High-Rise Martini
Michael Douglas in Wall Street

WHEN CORPORATE RAIDER GORDON GEKKO SAID, "GREED IS GOOD", HE WAS TALKING ABOUT MONEY. BUT HE COULD JUST AS EASILY HAVE BEEN TALKING ABOUT THIS POWERFUL COCKTAIL. ONE SIP AND YOU'LL WANT MORE, MORE, MORE.

Add the alcohols to an ice-filled highball glass (spirit first) and give the drink a gentle stir. Top up with your mixer of choice and garnish with a lemon, lime and orange peel to serve.

30 ml/1 oz. Mermaid Zest Gin or Adnams Rye Hill Vodka

1 barspoon dry vermouth

1 barspoon bianco vermouth

100 ml/3½ oz. sparkling water or sparkling lemonade/lemon soda

twist of lemon, lime and orange peel, to garnish

Serves 1

Espresso Martini
George Clooney

25 ml/¾ oz. freshly brewed strong espresso coffee

50 ml/1¾ oz. vodka

25 ml/¾ oz. Kahlúa or Tia Maria

½ tablespoon simple sugar syrup

3 coffee beans, to garnish (optional)

Serves 1

HAVING BEEN THE FACE OF NESPRESSO COFFEE FOR MORE THAN 15 YEARS, THE SMOOTH, RICH, CHARISMATIC GEORGE CLOONEY HAS A LOT IN COMMON WITH THIS UNBELIEVABLE, UNFORGETTABLE ESPRESSO MARTINI. *WHAT ELSE?*

Pour all the ingredients into a cocktail shaker filled with ice and shake vigorously. Strain into a martini glass. Wait for the cocktail to 'separate' – foam will rise to the top and the liquid below will become clearer. Garnish with coffee beans (if liked) and serve.

Breakfast Martini

Audrey Hepburn in Breakfast at Tiffany's

START YOUR DAY WITH A TANG WITH THIS VIBRANT BREAKFAST MARTINI, MIXED WITH SWEET MARMALADE. COME TO THINK OF IT, MARMALADE WOULD MAKE A GREAT NAME FOR THE FLIGHTY MISS GOLIGHTLY'S NAMELESS GINGER CAT.

Add the ingredients to a cocktail shaker and shake vigorously with ice. Fine-strain into a V-shaped cocktail glass and serve.

60 ml/2 oz.
Shortcross Gin

15 ml/½ oz. fresh
lemon juice

1 heaped teaspoon
good marmalade

Serves 1

French Martini
Brigitte Bardot

50 ml/1¾ oz. vodka

10 ml/⅓ oz. Chambord

75 ml/2½ oz. fresh
pineapple juice

pineapple wedges, to
garnish (optional)

Serves 1

WHEN ASKED WHAT THE BEST DAY OF HER LIFE WAS, FRENCH SCREEN GODDESS BRIGITTE BARDOT REPLIED, "IT WAS A NIGHT." CHANNEL THE SEDUCTIVE SEX KITTEN OF THE 1950S AND 1960S AS YOU BRING THIS FRUITY FRENCH MARTINI TO YOUR LIPS. OOH LA LA!

Pour all the ingredients into a cocktail shaker filled with ice cubes. Shake sharply and strain into a frosted martini glass or coupe glass. Garnish with pineapple wedges on a pick (if liked) and serve.

Remember Me Martini

Cary Grant in An Affair to Remember

THE SPICY CHILLI LIQUEUR IN THIS
MARTINI MAKES FOR AN UNFORGETTABLE
DRINK. JUST AS CARY GRANT AND
DEBORAH KERR PLANNING TO MEET AT
THE TOP OF THE EMPIRE STATE BUILDING
MADE FOR AN UNFORGETTABLE MOVIE
MOMENT, INSPIRING A NUMBER OF OTHER
FILMS, INCLUDING *SLEEPLESS IN SEATTLE*.

Add the ingredients to a cocktail shaker and
shake vigorously with ice. Fine-strain into a small
margarita glass and garnish with an olive and
a cocktail gherkin.

NOTE: The drink calls for Ancho Reyes Verde
Chile Liqueur, which was first made in Mexico in
1927. It is made using ancho and roasted poblano
chilli peppers and the result is a balanced, but
accessible, product that won't blow your head
off. It adds a deliciously subtle spiciness here.

40 ml/1½ oz. blanco
mezcal or tequila

15 ml/½ oz.
bianco vermouth

15 ml/½ oz. Ancho
Reyes Verde Chile
Liqueur or other
chilli/chile liqueur

10 ml/⅓ oz. fresh
lime juice

green olive and a
cocktail gherkin,
to garnish

Serves 1

CHAPTER 2

Oscar-Worthy Whiskey

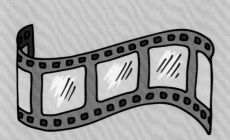

Whiskey Highball
Bill Murray in Lost in Translation

IN TOKYO TO PROMOTE SUNTORY
WHISKY, BILL MURRAY'S CHARACTER
IN *LOST IN TRANSLATION* IS YOUR
PERFECT DRINKING COMPANION FOR
THIS HIGHBALL, MADE WITH JAPANESE
WHISKEY. A MIDLIFE CRISIS HAS NEVER
TASTED SO GOOD.

60 ml/2 oz. Nikka
Taketsuru Pure
Malt Whiskey

soda water, to top up

twist of lemon zest
or fresh mint sprig,
to garnish

Serves 1

Fill a highball glass with large, clear ice cubes and
carefully pour the whisky down the side of the
glass so that it does not touch the top of the
ice. Add the soda slowly in the same manner
and stop filling once the soda reaches around
1 cm/½ inch from the top of the glass. Use a
barspoon to mix the whisky and soda by placing
the spoon between the ice and glass and moving
the spoon up and down or in a circular motion
for about 5–10 seconds. Serve without a straw.
Garnish with a twist of lemon zest or a mint
sprig to add aroma to the drink and serve.

Sweet Manhattan

Marilyn Monroe in Some Like it Hot

50 ml/1¾ oz. Jefferson's Reserve Bourbon

25 ml/¾ oz. Cocchi Vermouth di Torino or other sweet vermouth

3 dashes Angostura Bitters

twist of orange zest, to serve

Luxardo Maraschino Cherry, to garnish

Serves 1

CHANNEL SUGAR KANE KOWALCZYK IN *SOME LIKE IT HOT* BY USING A HOT-WATER BOTTLE AS A COCKTAIL SHAKER… THEN HAVE AN IMPROMPTU MANHATTAN PARTY, COMPLETE WITH "SPILLS, THRILLS, LAUGHS AND GAMES".

Combine all the drink ingredients in a mixing glass with a scoop of ice cubes. Stir for about 30 seconds before straining into a chilled coupette glass. Squeeze the orange zest to express the citrus oils over the drink and discard.

Garnish with a Luxardo Maraschino Cherry and serve.

Tipperary
Colin Farrell

50 ml/1¾ oz.
Teeling Whiskey

25 ml/¾ oz. Carpano
Antica Formula or other
sweet vermouth

10 ml/⅓ oz. Green
Chartreuse

2 dashes
Angostura Bitters

twist of orange zest,
to garnish

Serves 1

IT MAY BE A LONG WAY TO TIPPERARY
BUT IT'S ONLY A FEW SHORT SIPS TO
DESTINATION DELICIOUS WITH THIS
IRISH-WHISKEY COCKTAIL, NAMED AFTER
THE TOWN A COUPLE OF HOURS
FROM COLIN FARRELL'S BIRTHPLACE
OF CASTLEKNOCK. GRAND!

Combine all the drink ingredients in a mixing
glass with a scoop of ice cubes. Stir for
30 seconds before straining into a chilled
coupette glass. Squeeze the orange zest to
express the citrus oils over the drink before
adding as a garnish to the glass. Serve.

Lion's Tail

James Earl Jones in
The Lion King

RAISE A GLASS OF THIS SPICY, HERBACEOUS
COCKTAIL AS YOU LISTEN TO THE
COMMANDING VOICE OF MUFASA EXPLAIN
ALL ABOUT THE CIRCLE OF LIFE TO HIS
PLAYFUL CUB, SIMBA. HAKUNA MATATA!

45 ml/1½ oz. Wild
Turkey 80 Proof Bourbon

25 ml/¾ oz. fresh lime juice

3½ teaspoons simple sugar syrup

10 ml/⅓ oz. Yellow Chartreuse

5 dashes The Bitter Truth Pimento Dram

twist of lime zest, to garnish

Serves 1

Combine all the drink ingredients in a cocktail
shaker with a scoop of ice cubes and shake hard.
Strain into a chilled coupe glass and garnish with
a twist of lime zest. Serve.

CHAPTER 3

Tinseltown Tequila

Smoking President

Kevin Costner in JFK

KNOWN TO ENJOY A CUBAN CIGAR, PRESIDENT JOHN F. KENNEDY WAS ASSASSINATED ON 22 NOVEMBER, 1963. WATCH KEVIN COSTNER TRY TO EXPOSE THE TRUTH ABOUT THAT FATEFUL DAY AS THE "WHITE IS BLACK, AND BLACK IS WHITE" DISTRICT ATTORNEY IN THE GRIPPING *JFK*.

Stir all the drink ingredients over ice cubes in a rocks glass for 30–40 seconds, or until the desired level of dilution is reached. Gently squeeze the lemon zest garnish to express the citrus oils into the glass. Garnish the glass with the lemon zest and a lavender sprig. Serve.

60 ml/2 oz.
Los Danzantes
Reposado Mezcal

5 ml/¼ oz.
agave nectar

2 dashes Bob's
Lavender Bitters

2 dashes Bob's
Cardamom Bitters

twist of lemon zest and
fresh lavender sprig,
to garnish

Serves 1

El Diablo

Meryl Streep in The Devil Wears Prada

50 ml/1¾ oz. Ocho
Blanco Tequila

25 ml/¾ oz. fresh
lime juice

10 ml/⅓ oz. fresh
ginger juice

4 teaspoons simple
sugar syrup

10 ml/⅓ oz. Merlet
Crème de Cassis

Fever-Tree Ginger Ale,
to top up

lime wedge, to garnish

Serves 1

FIERCE, FIERY AND FAH-BU-LOUS, THIS
RUTHLESS COCKTAIL HAS A LOT IN
COMMON WITH THE EDITOR-IN-CHIEF OF
RUNWAY MAGAZINE. THE WITH-A-KICK MIX
OF TEQUILA, LIME, GINGER AND CRÈME DE
CASSIS WILL NEVER GO OUT OF STYLE.

Add all the drink ingredients, except the ginger
ale, to a cocktail shaker with ice, then shake
hard. Strain into a highball glass (over ice cubes
if preferred) and top up with ginger ale. Garnish
with a lime wedge and serve.

Vampire's Kiss

Brad Pitt in Interview with the Vampire

FEELING (BLOOD)THIRSTY? SINK YOUR TEETH INTO THIS SPINE-CHILLING COCKTAIL AS YOU WATCH THE 11-YEAR-OLD KIRSTEN DUNST GIVE FELLOW VAMPIRE BRAD PITT A CREEPY, IMMORTAL KISS. A TO-DIE-FOR DRINK WITH SERIOUS BITE.

40 ml/1½ oz. Reposado Tequila

20 ml/⅔ oz. amontillado sherry

20 ml/⅔ oz. blood orange juice

1 tablespoon simple sugar syrup

grapefruit peel fangs, to garnish (optional)

Serves 1

Add the ingredients to a cocktail shaker and shake vigorously with ice. Fine-strain into a coupe glass, garnish with grapefruit fangs and serve.

To make the grapefruit fang garnish: Use a vegetable peeler to slice a large piece of grapefruit peel (4 × 7.5 cm/1½ × 3 in.). Use a sharp knife to carefully cut a jagged zig-zag to form the fangs on one end.

NOTE: Amontillado sherry is ideal for this cocktail and was a favourite of horror writer Edgar Allen Poe. Cream or sweet sherry also works, but you may want to omit the additional sugar syrup.

Watermelon Rosé Margarita
Jennifer Grey in Dirty Dancing

500 g/1 lb. 2 oz. fresh
watermelon flesh, deseeded
and cubed

lime wedge and salt, to rim
the glass

60 ml/2 oz. tequila blanco

45 ml/1½ oz. triple sec

30 ml/1 oz. fresh lime juice

60 ml/2 oz. Watermelon &
Rosé Syrup (see below)

60 ml/2 oz. sweet, fruity
rosé wine, well chilled
(a Californian Zinfandel
works well here)

lime wedges and
watermelon slices,
to garnish

Serves 2-4

SHE CARRIED A WATERMELON (*CRINGE*).
THEN SHE DID SOME DIRTY DANCING. THEN
SHE ROCKED JOHNNY CASTLE'S WORLD, JUST
AS THIS REFRESHING MARGARITA IS SURE TO
ROCK YOURS.

Put the watermelon cubes in a blender and blend
until puréed. Strain the liquid through a fine-mesh
sieve/strainer into a jug/pitcher. Discard the pulp and
seeds; reserve the juice. Place some salt on a plate.
Rim the glass with a lime wedge, then dip the glass
into the salt to coat. Discard the lime wedge. Pop
the glass in the freezer to chill until needed.

Add the tequila, triple sec, lime juice, syrup, rosé
wine and 60 ml/2 oz. of the watermelon juice to
an ice-filled cocktail shaker. Shake until cold, about
20 seconds. Pour into the prepared glasses. Garnish
with a lime wedge and a watermelon slice. Serve.

125 ml/4 oz. sweet, fruity
rosé wine

125 ml/4 oz. fresh
watermelon juice (see
method above)

250 g/9 oz. white sugar

Watermelon & Rosé Syrup

Combine the rosé, watermelon juice and sugar in a
saucepan over a medium heat. Bring to the boil,
whisking until the sugar dissolves. Turn off the heat
and let the mixture cool to room temperature. Strain
into a clean screw-top jar to store until required.

Pink Chihuahua

Reese Witherspoon in Legally Blonde

BEND AND SNAP YOUR WAY TO THIS
BLUSHING COCKTAIL, WHICH COMBINES
TWO OF ELLE WOODS' FAVOURITE
THINGS: THE COLOUR PINK AND HER
BELOVED HANDBAG-SIZE CHIHUAHUA,
NAMED BRUISER. THE VERDICT? YUMMY.

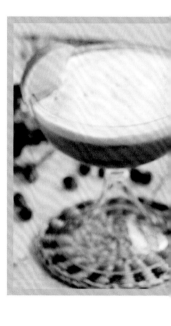

50 ml/1¾ oz. Olmeca Altos Plata Tequila

25 ml/¾ oz. fresh pomegranate juice

25 ml/¾ oz. fresh lime juice

20 ml/⅔ oz. orgeat

10 ml/⅓ oz. egg white

lime wedge, to garnish

Serves 1

Add all the drink ingredients to a cocktail shaker
and 'dry' shake first without ice. Add ice cubes
and shake a second time. Strain into a chilled
coupe glass. Garnish with a lime wedge on the
rim of the glass and serve.

CHAPTER 4

Glitterati Gin

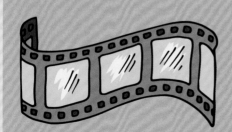

Turbo G&T

Vin Diesel in Fast & Furious

GO FROM ZERO TO 100 WITH THIS
EXPLOSIVE COCKTAIL, GUARANTEED
TO TURBO-CHARGE YOUR TASTE BUDS.
TOUGH GUY VIN DIESEL – AND HIS BICEPS
– WOULD SURELY APPROVE. PEDAL TO
THE METAL.

Add the ingredients to a cocktail shaker and
shake vigorously with ice. Fine-strain into a
V-shaped cocktail glass and garnish with a lime
wheel, if you like. Serve.

60 ml/2 oz. Hayman's
London Dry Gin or
other classic gin

10 ml/¼ oz. fresh
lime juice

10 ml/¼ oz.
tonic water syrup

2–3 dashes
orange bitters

lime wheel, to garnish
(optional)

Serves 1

Red-Hot Negroni

Sir Michael Caine in The Italian Job

25 ml/¾ oz. Ableforth's Bathtub Gin

25 ml/¾ oz. red vermouth

25 ml/¾ oz. Campari

125 ml/4 oz. freshly brewed red berry tea, hot

raspberries and an orange wheel, to garnish

Serves 1

HAILING FROM ITALY BUT SERVED IN A BRITISH TEAPOT, THIS RED-HOT NEGRONI IS THE PERFECT ACCOMPANIMENT TO WATCHING SIR MICHAEL CAINE'S CHARACTER DEADPAN: "YOU'RE ONLY SUPPOSED TO BLOW THE BLOODY DOORS OFF" IN COMIC CAPER MOVIE *THE ITALIAN JOB*.

Add the gin, vermouth and Campari to a pre-heated latte glass (this keeps the drink hotter for longer) and stir. Top up with the red berry tea and stir again. Garnish with raspberries and orange peel. Serve hot.

Casablanca
Humphrey Bogart
in Casablanca

"OF ALL THE GIN JOINTS IN ALL THE TOWNS IN ALL THE WORLD, SHE WALKS INTO MINE." SO SAID AN ANGUISHED HUMPHREY BOGART IN THE CLASSIC ROMANTIC DRAMA *CASABLANCA*. CREATE YOUR VERY OWN GIN JOINT, SERVING THIS BUBBLY BEVERAGE AS THE SIGNATURE COCKTAIL.

1 egg white

50 ml/1¾ oz. gin

25 ml/¾ oz. fresh lemon juice

1 barspoon sugar or 1 tablespoon simple sugar syrup

Champagne, to top up

Serves 1

Put the egg white, gin, lemon juice and sugar into an ice-filled shaker and shake vigorously. Strain into a collins or highball glass filled with ice cubes. Top up with Champagne and serve.

Ultimate Pink Negroni

Margo Robbie in Barbie

25 ml/¾ oz. Mermaid
Pink Gin

25 ml/¾ oz. Aperol

25 ml/¾ oz.
rosé vermouth
(such as Belsazar Rosé
or Mancino Sakura)

strawberry and
raspberry, to garnish

Serves 1

PINK HOUSE, PINK HEELS, PINK CLOTHES, PINK CAR, PINK RECORD PLAYER, PINK SUNLOUNGERS, PINK BED, PINK SHOWER, PINK CAMPERVAN, PINK BOAT, PINK BBQ, PINK-CLAD BOYFRIEND… HECK, BARBIE'S WHOLE PERFECT WORLD IS PINK! WHAT BETTER COCKTAIL TO ACCOMPANY THE ROSY DOLL?

Add the ingredients to an ice-filled mixing glass and stir. Strain into a coupe glass. Garnish with a strawberry and a raspberry threaded onto a cocktail pick. Serve.

Cake it to the Limit
Kirsten Dunst in Marie Antoinette

BEST SIPPED LUXURIATING IN A DEEP
BATHTUB WHILE WEARING DIAMONDS
AND DECLARING, "LET THEM EAT CAKE"
– À LA KIRSTEN DUNST AS MARIE
ANTOINETTE – THIS ZINGY COCKTAIL
WILL INSPIRE ALL THE DECADENCE,
SCANDAL AND ARTISTIC TENDENCIES
OF THE QUEEN OF FRANCE HERSELF.

caster/superfine sugar,
for the glass

45 ml/1½ oz. citrus
gin (such as Sipsmith
Lemon Drizzle)

30 ml/1 oz. Frangelico

10 ml/⅓ oz. fresh
lemon juice

twist of lemon zest,
to garnish

Serves 1

Sprinkle a little sugar on a plate. Wet the rim of
a chilled cocktail glass and dip it in the sugar
to rim. Set aside.

Add the ingredients to a cocktail shaker with
ice cubes and shake. Strain into the rimmed
glass. Garnish with a lemon zest and serve.

Fascinator

Katherine Heigl in 27 Dresses

45 ml/1½ oz. Japanese gin (such as Roku)

20 ml/⅔ oz. Mancino Sakura Vermouth or dry vermouth

1 barspoon elderflower cordial

2–3 dashes Absinthe

mint leaves, to garnish

Serves 1

WHO DOESN'T LOVE A WEDDING (WHILST DONNING A FANCY HEADPIECE)? WELL, BY HER 27TH AS BRIDESMAID – WEARING ALL MANNER OF RIDICULOUS GET-UPS – KATHERINE HEIGL IS A BIT OVER THEM! A FEW FASCINATORS SERVED BY A HOT BARMAN, HOWEVER, WOULD LIKELY MAKE THE 28TH ALL THE MORE BEARABLE.

Add the ingredients to a mixing glass and stir with ice. Strain into a chilled coupe glass and garnish with a few mint leaves.

Chardonnay Cocktail

Renée Zellweger in Bridget Jones' Diary

JUST AS MARK DARCY DECLARES, "I LIKE YOU VERY MUCH – JUST AS YOU ARE," TO OUR DUMBSTRUCK HEROINE BRIDGET JONES, YOU'LL LIKE THIS REFRESHING CHARDONNAY COCKTAIL VERY MUCH, JUST AS IT IS. BIG KNICKERS OPTIONAL (BUT HIGHLY RECOMMENDED).

100 ml/3½ oz. Chardonnay wine, chilled

15 ml/1 tablespoon London dry gin

3 tbsp Cucumber Simple Syrup (see below)

juice of 1 lime

frozen slices of cucumber, to garnish

Serves 1

In a large ice-filled wine glass, combine the Chardonnay, gin, Cucumber Simple Syrup and lime juice. Stir, garnish with frozen cucumber slices and serve at once.

Cucumber Simple Syrup

250 ml/9 oz. granulated sugar

1 cucumber, peeled and sliced

Combine the sugar with 250 ml/9 oz. water in a saucepan. Bring to the boil, stirring until the sugar is dissolved. Turn off the heat and add the cucumber slices. Let sit at room temperature for 15 minutes, then strain.

Charlie Chaplin

Robert Downey Jr

in Chaplin

THE KING OF CINEMA'S SILENT ERA,
CHARLIE CHAPLIN WAS PORTRAYED
TO PERFECTION BY ROBERT DOWNEY JR.
IN THE OSCAR-NOMINATED *CHAPLIN*.
NAMED AFTER THE ICONIC SLAPSTICK
ACTOR AND FILMMAKER, YOU'LL BE
FALLING OVER YOURSELF TO GET A TASTE
OF THIS SWEET 'N' SOUR COCKTAIL.

25 ml/¾ oz. De Kuyper Apricot
Brandy Liqueur

25 ml/¾ oz.
Hayman's Sloe Gin

25 ml/¾ oz. fresh lime juice

10 ml/⅓ oz. water, chilled
(omit if using wet ice)

Serves 1

Shake all the ingredients with ice cubes in
a cocktail shaker and fine-strain into a chilled
coupe glass to serve.

Appletini
Matt Damon in Good Will Hunting

45 ml/1½ oz. gin (or vodka if preferred)

25 ml/¾ oz. fresh lemon juice

20 ml/⅔ oz. sour apple liqueur or green apple schnapps

1½ tablespoons simple sugar syrup

green apple slice or fan, to garnish

Serves 1

"DO YOU LIKE APPLES? WELL, I GOT HER NUMBER. HOW DO YOU LIKE THEM APPLES?!" SO SAID WILL TO A COCKY COLLEGE STUDENT AFTER GETTING SKYLAR'S PHONE NUMBER IN *GOOD WILL HUNTING*. IF YOU LIKE APPLES – AND SEEING MATT DAMON NAILING HIS BREAKTHROUGH ROLE – YOU'LL LOVE THIS CRISP, CONFIDENT COCKTAIL.

Add all the ingredients to a cocktail shaker with ice cubes. Shake vigorously and strain into a chilled martini glass. Garnish with an apple slice or fan and serve.

CHAPTER 5

Lights, Vodka, Action

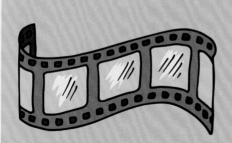

Stinger

Robert Redford in The Sting

WATCH ROBERT REDFORD AND HIS PAL
PAUL NEWMAN LIE, CHEAT, GAMBLE AND
SWINDLE THEIR WAY TO THE BIG STING
WITH THIS CONFIDENT COCKTAIL IN
HAND, FIT FOR THE MOST CHARMING
OF CONMEN. MAKE IT WITH VODKA OR
UP YOUR GAME AND OPT FOR BRANDY!

Add the ingredients to a cocktail shaker with
ice and shake vigorously. Strain into an ice-filled
tumbler or rocks glass. Garnish with a mint sprig
and serve.

**60 ml/2 oz. vodka
or brandy**

**25 ml/¾ oz. white
crème de menthe**

mint sprig, to garnish

Serves 1

Prosecco Mary

Cameron Diaz in
There's Something About Mary

30 ml/1 oz. vodka

75 ml/2½ oz. tomato juice

a dash Tabasco hot sauce

a pinch of sugar

¼ teaspoon smoked water (optional)

about 75 ml/2½ oz. Prosecco, chilled

cucumber ribbons, to garnish (see Note)

Serves 1

THERE'S SOMETHING ABOUT MARY… AND THERE'S ALSO SOMETHING ABOUT THIS VARIATION ON THE CLASSIC BLOODY MARY. QUAFF THE KOOKY BEVERAGE AS YOU CHUCKLE ALONG WITH THIS 'HAIR-RAISING' SCREWBALL COMEDY.

Pour the vodka, tomato juice, Tabasco, sugar and smoked water (if liked), into a cocktail shaker half-filled with ice cubes. Shake vigorously and pour into a flute or rocks glass. Add half the Prosecco and stir gently to combine. Top up with the rest of the Prosecco, add some cucumber ribbons down the side of the glass to garnish and serve.

NOTE: Use a vegetable peeler to make the cucumber ribbon garnish.

Cosmopolitan

Sarah Jessica Parker in Sex and the City

IN THE WORLD OF CARRIE BRADSHAW AND HER THREE BESTIES, THERE ARE HIGHS, THERE ARE LOWS, AND THERE ARE OH-SO-MANY ZESTY PINK COCKTAILS. GATHER YOUR GIRLS AND RAISE YOUR COSMOS TO FRIENDSHIP, FINDING LOVE AND MANOLO BLAHNIKS.

35 ml/1¼ oz. lemon vodka

20 ml/⅔ oz. triple sec

20 ml/⅔ oz. fresh lime juice

25 ml/¾ oz. cranberry juice

flamed orange zest, to garnish (see Note)

Serves 1

Add all the ingredients to a cocktail shaker filled with ice cubes, shake sharply and strain into a chilled martini glass. Garnish with flamed orange zest and serve.

NOTE: To add a flamed orange zest, squeeze the citrus oils from a large strip of orange zest, while holding it skin downwards over a flame, set above the cocktail. Rub the rim of the glass with the flamed orange zest before using it to garnish the drink.

Moscow Mule
Scarlett Johansson in Black Widow

50 ml/1¾ oz. vodka

1 lime, quartered

spicy ginger beer, chilled, to top up

Serves 1

A RUSSIAN AGENT TRAINED AS AN ASSASSIN, SPY, MARTIAL ARTIST AND ALL-ROUND BADASS, THE MOSCOW MULE IS THE ULTIMATE SPICY REFRESHMENT FOR BLACK WIDOW TO DEVOUR AFTER SHE'S RELEASED HER ELECTRIFYING 'WIDOW'S BITE'.

Add the vodka to a copper tankard or highball glass filled with crushed ice. Squeeze over the lime wedges and drop the spent husks in too. Top up with ginger beer, stir gently and serve.

White Russian

Jeff Bridges in The Big Lebowski

WHAT TO DO WHEN YOU'RE BEING ATTACKED BY GOONS, STALKED BY GERMAN NIHILISTS AND KIDNAPPED BY A PORN KINGPIN? MAKE LIKE THE DUDE AND WHIP YOURSELF UP A WHITE RUSSIAN. THEN HIT THE BOWLING ALLEY.

50 ml/1¾ oz. vodka

25 ml/¾ oz. Kahlúa

25 ml/¾ oz. single/light cream, chilled

stemmed cocktail cherry, to garnish (optional)

Serves 1

Combine the vodka and Kahlúa in a mixing glass with a handful of ice cubes. Stir to chill and strain into a rocks glass filled with fresh ice cubes. Layer the chilled cream into the glass over the back of a long-handled barspoon. Garnish with a stemmed cherry, if liked, and serve.

Bay Breeze

Keira Knightley in Pirates of the Caribbean

60 ml/2 oz. vodka

45 ml/1½ oz. cranberry juice

75 ml/2½ oz. fresh pineapple juice

soda water, chilled, to top up (optional)

pineapple wedge and leaf, to garnish

Serves 1

SWASHBUCKLING SWORD FIGHTS… SINKING SHIPS… PIRATE GHOSTS… MIX UP THIS DEATHLY DELICIOUS DRINK, THEN SET SAIL WITH KEIRA KNIGHTLEY AND HER COMRADES ON AN EPIC ADVENTURE ACROSS THE HAUNTED SHORES. LESS A BREEZE; MORE A RAGING SQUALL.

Combine all the ingredients in a mixing glass filled with ice cubes. Stir to chill and pour into a highball glass filled with fresh ice cubes. Top up with a splash of chilled soda for a lighter drink (if liked). Garnish with a pineapple wedge and leaf and serve.

Purple Haze

Whoopi Goldberg in The Color Purple

WITH 11 OSCAR NOMINATIONS (INCLUDING BEST ACTRESS IN A LEADING ROLE FOR WHOOPI GOLDBERG), *THE COLOR PURPLE* WILL HAVE YOU WEEPING INTO YOUR PURPLE HAZE AS YOU WATCH THE BRAVE CELIE OVERCOME CRUELTY, POVERTY AND RACISM. HANKIES AT THE READY.

45 ml/1½ oz. vodka

30 ml/1 oz. Chambord

lime soda or sparkling clear lemonade/lemon soda, chilled, to top up

raspberries, lime wedge and mint leaves, to garnish

Serves 1

Pour the vodka and Chambord into a cocktail shaker and add a handful of ice cubes. Shake well and strain into an ice-filled rocks glass. Top up with lime soda or lemonade, garnish with raspberries, a lime wedge and mint leaves, and serve.

Gotham Martini

Christian Bale in The Dark Knight

60 ml/2 oz. Stolichnaya
Vodka, frozen

a dash of black sambuca

Serves 1

DARK, BROODING AND MYSTERIOUS,
THIS ENIGMATIC COCKTAIL EXUDES
SUPERHERO STATUS. ADD MORE BLACK
SAMBUCA TO FEEL ONE STEP CLOSER TO
THE LEGENDARY BATMAN AND HIS CITY
OF GOTHAM.

Pour the frozen vodka into a chilled martini
glass, gently add the sambuca but do not stir or
mix as you want to preserve the cloudy effect.
Serve.

Silver Streak

Gene Wilder in Silver Streak

LOVE, MURDER AND A HIGH-SPEED
TRAIN THAT GENE WILDER GETS
THROWN FROM ARE A RECIPE FOR
ADVENTURE AND GIGGLES GALORE
IN THE 1976 COMEDY *SILVER STREAK*.
VODKA AND THE UNUSUAL KÜMMEL
LIQUEUR ARE A RECIPE FOR THE PERFECT
AFTER-DINNER NIGHTCAP.

Pour the vodka into a rocks glass filled with
ice cubes. Add the Kümmel, stir gently to chill
and serve.

25 ml/¾ oz. vodka,
chilled

25 ml/¾ oz.
Kümmel Liqueur

Serves 1

CHAPTER 6

Roll 'Em
Rum

Tiki Negroni

Dwayne Johnson in Moana

THIS TRANSFORMATIVE COCKTAIL WITH POLYNESIAN VIBES IS FIT FOR AN INKED-UP, SHAPESHIFTING DEMIGOD… OR, INDEED, YOU. PULL UP A PALM TREE, CHANNEL *MOANA'S* MASSIVE MAUI AND DRIFT AWAY ON A SEA OF FRUITY RUM. YOU'RE WELCOME.

Add the ingredients to an ice-filled cocktail shaker and shake vigorously. Fine-strain into an ice-filled rocks glass and garnish with a lime wheel, pineapple wedge and pineapple leaves to serve.

25 ml/¾ oz.
Citadelle Gin

25 ml/¾ oz.
red vermouth

25 ml/¾ oz. Campari

25 ml/¾ oz. Plantation
Pineapple Rum

3–4 dashes
Angostura Bitters

lime wheel, small
pineapple wedge and
pineapple leaves,
to garnish

Serves 1

Miami Vice

Jamie Foxx in Miami Vice

1 x 250-ml/9-oz. can premixed strawberry daiquiri

30 ml/1 oz. white rum

1 x 250-ml/9-oz. can premixed piña colada

Serves 2

COOL OFF WITH THIS CHILLED TWO-LAYERED RUM COCKTAIL AFTER WATCHING JAMIE FOXX AND HIS UNDERCOVER-COP PARTNER SAVE THE DAY, VIA SHOOT-UPS, DRUG RAIDS AND HIGH-SPEED BOAT RIDES. AN '80S CLASSIC REINVENTED WITH STYLE.

Blend the strawberry daiquiri with ice and half of the white rum until it forms a smooth slush. Pour into a hurricane glass.

Next, blend the piña colada with ice and the rest of the rum. Pour into the same hurricane glass on top of the strawberry daiquiri slush, creating a layering effect. Serve at once with a straw.

NOTE: If you prefer, you can make the piña colada and strawberry daiquiri from scratch using your preferred recipes and then blend them.

Something Blue
Elvis Presley in Blue Hawaii

WAVES CRASHING… PALM TREES SWAYING IN THE BREEZE… ELVIS CROONING WHILST PLAYING A UKULELE… THERE'S ONLY ONE THING MISSING FROM THIS PICTURE OF PARADISE: A TROPICAL, FRUITY COCKTAIL. DIG OUT YOUR GRASS SKIRT AND FIX IT.

Add the ingredients, apart from the blue Curaçao, to a cocktail shaker with ice and shake vigorously. Pour into an ice-filled hurricane glass, or similar. Pour the blue Curaçao down the inside of the glass – it will sink, creating the layered effect. Garnish with pineapple wedges and serve.

30 ml/1 oz. coconut rum

25 ml/¾ oz. vanilla vodka

45 ml/1½ oz. pineapple juice

10 ml/⅓ oz. amaretto

15 ml/½ oz. fresh lime juice

10 ml/⅓ oz. blue Curaçao

pineapple wedges, to garnish

Serves 1

Twisted Pineapple Frosé

Seth Rogan in Pineapple Express

1 x 750-ml/25-oz. bottle full-flavoured, full-bodied rosé wine (a Pinot Noir or Merlot works well here)

250 ml/9 oz. fresh pineapple juice

45 ml/1½ oz. Bacardi

2 tablespoons simple sugar syrup

30 ml/1 oz. fresh lime juice

½ fresh red chilli/chile, deseeded and finely chopped, plus extra to garnish (optional)

pineapple leaf and/ or pineapple wedge, to garnish

Serves 3-4

ALL ABOARD THE PINEAPPLE EXPRESS WITH THIS SWEET, FRUITY NUMBER. SIP AWAY AS YOU WATCH SETH ROGAN AND JAMES FRANCO RUNNING FOR THEIR LIVES IN THIS STONER ACTION COMEDY. THUG LIFE ISN'T ALL IT'S CRACKED UP TO BE… BUT THIS COCKTAIL IS.

Pour the rosé and pineapple juice into a freezerproof container. Stir to mix and freeze until solid. Remove from the freezer and allow it to defrost for 35–40 minutes until you can break it up with a fork but it's still holding plenty of ice crystals.

Scoop into the cup of a blender and add the Bacardi, sugar syrup, lime juice and chilli. Blend for about 30 seconds until foamy and speckled with red chilli.

Spoon into serving glasses, add a pineapple leaf and/or a pineapple wedge and a sprinkling of red chilli to garnish (optional). Serve with straws.

Daredevil
Tom Cruise in
Mission: Impossible

DRIVING A MOTORBIKE OFF A CLIFF…
CLIMBING UP THE WORLD'S TALLEST
BUILDING… HANGING ON TO A SHEER
ROCK FACE WITH HIS BARE HANDS…
THE STUNTS IN THE *MISSION: IMPOSSIBLE*
FILMS DON'T GET MUCH MORE DARING
– AND GUTSY TOM CRUISE DOES MOST
OF THEM HIMSELF!

Build the cocktail over ice in a highball glass
in the order the ingredients are listed. Add
a swizzle stick and garnish with a mint sprig
and/or red berries to serve.

30 ml/1 oz. 151
(over-proof) rum

150 ml/5 oz. fresh
orange juice

70 ml/2½ oz.
unsweetened
cranberry juice

70 ml/2½ oz. fresh
pineapple juice

15 ml/½ oz. Myer's
Dark Rum

a splash of sparkling
lemonade/lemon soda

mint sprig and/or red
berries, to garnish

Serves 1

Dramatic
Desserts

Negroni Float

Angelina Jolie in Girl, Interrupted

ANGELINA JOLIE'S CHARACTER CAUSES QUITE A STIR WHEN SHE ORDERS A VANILLA SUNDAE WITH HOT FUDGE DURING AN OUTING TO THE ICE CREAM PARLOUR. SHE REQUESTS SPRINKLES ("RAINBOW, NOT CHOCOLATE"), WHIPPED CREAM AND CHERRIES. SO SHE'D SURELY GIVE THIS NEGRONI FLOAT THE THUMBS-UP.

15 ml/½ oz. Campfire Navy Gin

15 ml/½ oz. Campari

15 ml/½ oz. red vermouth

1 scoop vanilla ice cream

100 ml/3½ oz. cola, chilled

whipped cream, sprinkles and a fresh cherry, to garnish

Serves 1

Half-fill a large, tall glass with ice and add the gin, Campari, red vermouth and ice cream before carefully (and slowly) topping up with chilled cola.

Garnish with whipped cream, rainbow sprinkles and a cherry. Serve with a straw.

VARIATION: This recipe calls for classic vanilla ice cream, but you can have fun experimenting with different flavours – blood orange sorbet works rather well.

Queen of Hearts

Helena Bonham Carter
in Alice in Wonderland

5 ripe fresh
strawberries, hulled

75 ml/2½ oz. vodka

1 tablespoon simple
sugar syrup

5 ml/¼ oz. good aged
balsamic vinegar

edible flower, such
as a viola, and a
strawberry, to garnish

Serves 1

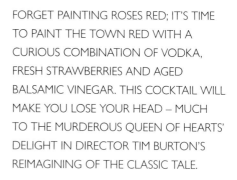

FORGET PAINTING ROSES RED; IT'S TIME TO PAINT THE TOWN RED WITH A CURIOUS COMBINATION OF VODKA, FRESH STRAWBERRIES AND AGED BALSAMIC VINEGAR. THIS COCKTAIL WILL MAKE YOU LOSE YOUR HEAD – MUCH TO THE MURDEROUS QUEEN OF HEARTS' DELIGHT IN DIRECTOR TIM BURTON'S REIMAGINING OF THE CLASSIC TALE.

Put four of the strawberries in a cocktail shaker and muddle to a pulp. Pour in all the remaining ingredients and add a handful of ice cubes. Shake well and strain into a coupe glass. Garnish with the remaining strawberry on a toothpick and an edible flower. Serve.

Turkish Martini

Tilda Swinton in
The Chronicles of Narnia

VENTURE INTO A FANTASTICAL WORLD OF CAVERNOUS WARDROBES AND TALKING LIONS WITH THIS TEMPTING TIPPLE. JUST AS EDMUND COULDN'T RESIST THE LURE OF TURKISH DELIGHT OFFERED BY THE WHITE WITCH, YOU WON'T BE ABLE TO RESIST THIS COMBINATION OF SWEET CRÈME DE CACAO AND FRAGRANT ROSEWATER.

Dust a plate with cocoa powder. Wet the rim of a chilled martini glass and dip it in the cocoa to rim.

Add the vodka, white crème de cacao and rosewater to a cocktail shaker filled with ice cubes and shake well. Strain into the prepared glass, garnish with a candied rhubarb ribbon (if liked) and serve.

cocoa powder,
for the glass

50 ml/1¾ oz. vodka

5 ml/¼ oz. white crème
de cacao

2 dashes rosewater

candied rhubarb
ribbons, to garnish
(optional)

Serves 1

Banoffee & Lemon
Meringue Pie Cocktails
Keri Russell in Waitress

DESCRIBED AS A 'PIE GENIUS', THE PREGNANT, UNHAPPILY
MARRIED JENNA ASSERTS: "I DON'T NEED NO BABY,
I DON'T WANT NO TROUBLE, I JUST WANT TO MAKE PIES."
SHOW THE CONFLICTED WAITRESS SOME SOLIDARITY
AS YOU CONCOCT THESE DREAMY DESSERT COCKTAILS.

Banoffee pie

½ ripe banana, plus extra sliced
banana to garnish

45 ml/1½ oz. vanilla vodka

15 ml/½ oz. banana liqueur

10 ml/⅓ oz. caramel syrup, such
as Monin

15 ml/½ oz. fresh milk

whipped cream and grated dark
chocolate, to garnish

Serves 1

Muddle the banana in a cocktail
shaker, then add the other
ingredients. Shake vigorously with
ice and strain into a cocktail glass.
Garnish with whipped cream,
banana slices and grated chocolate.
Serve at once.

Lemon meringue pie

45 ml/1½ oz. gin

1 tablespoon lemon curd

15 ml/½ oz. limoncello

crushed meringue, to garnish

Serves 1

Add the ingredients to a cocktail
shaker with ice cubes. Shake
vigorously and strain into a cocktail
glass. Garnish with crushed
meringue and serve at once.

Chocolatini

Juliette Binoche in Chocolat

90 ml/3 oz. Bailey's Irish Cream Liqueur

30 ml/1 oz. dark crème de cacao

15 ml/½ oz. vodka

dark chocolate shavings, to garnish

Serves 1

BE SCANDALIZED YET DELIGHTED BY THIS DECADENT DESSERT COCKTAIL, JUST AS THE FOLK OF THE SMALL FRENCH VILLAGE IN *CHOCOLAT* ARE WHEN A NEW CHOCOLATERIE OPENS UP, SERVING UP LAUGHS, ROMANCE AND SINFUL CONFECTIONERY. AS DREAMY AS IT IS CREAMY.

Pour all the ingredients into a cocktail shaker, add a handful of ice cubes and shake until frosted. Strain into a chilled martini glass, sprinkle with dark chocolate shavings and serve.

Cleopatra

Elizabeth Taylor
in Cleopatra

SAID TO HAVE BATHED IN DONKEY'S
MILK TO MAINTAIN HER YOUTHFUL
COMPLEXION, THE EGYPTIAN QUEEN'S
COCKTAIL CALLS FOR COW'S MILK
INSTEAD. A LAVISH TIPPLE FIT FOR THE
'SIREN OF THE NILE'.

30 ml/1 oz. Bourbon

20 ml/⅔ oz. sweet vermouth

50 ml/1¾ oz. semi-skimmed milk

10 ml/⅓ oz. Luxardo Maraschino
Cherry Liqueur

Serves 1

Add the ingredients to a cocktail shaker with
ice cubes and shake vigorously. Fine-strain into
a stemmed cocktail glass and serve.

Snowball

Will Ferrell in Elf

35 ml/1¼ oz. Advocaat

10 ml/⅓ oz. lime cordial (optional)

120 ml/4 oz. clear sparkling lemonade

lime slice, cocktail cherry and mint leaf, to garnish

Serves 1

SON OF A NUTCRACKER – THIS CREAMY FESTIVE COCKTAIL IS SCRUMPTIOUS! UNLIKE THE ARSENAL OF SNOWBALLS BUDDY FIRES TO PROTECT HIS YOUNGER BROTHER FROM SNOW-LAUNCHING BULLIES, THE ONLY PLACE YOU'LL WANT TO THROW THIS SNOWBALL IS DOWN YOUR NECK.

Add the Advocaat and lime cordial (if using) to a highball glass filled with ice cubes. Top up with lemonade. Garnish with a slice of lime, a cocktail cherry and a mint leaf to serve.

INDEX

RECIPE CREDITS

David T. Smith & Keli Rivers
Banoffee Pie, Breakfast Martini, Cake it to the Limit, Cleopatra, Dirty Martini, Fascinator Martini, High-Rise Martini, Lemon Meringue Pie, Miami Vice, Millionaire's Martini, Negroni Float, Pornstar Martini, Red Hot Negroni, Remember Me Martini, Snowball, Something Blue, Stinger Turbo G&T, Ultimate Pink Negroni, Vampire's Kiss, Vesper Martini

Julia Charles
Appletini, Casablanca, Chardonnay Cocktail, Charlie Chaplin, Chocolatini, Daredevil, Espresso Martini, Purple Haze, Twisted Pineapple Frosé, Watermelon Rosé Margarita

Jesse Estes
El Diablo, Lion's Tail, Pink Chihuahua, Smoking President, Sweet Manhattan, Tipperary, Whiskey Highball

Ben Reed
Bay Breeze, Cosmopolitan, French Martini, Gotham Martini, Moscow Mule, Silver Streak, Turkish Martini, White Russian

Ursula Ferrigno
Queen of Hearts

Laura Gladwin
Prosecco Mary